What Did You Bring?

Written by Joanna Austin
Illustrated by Judy Moffatt

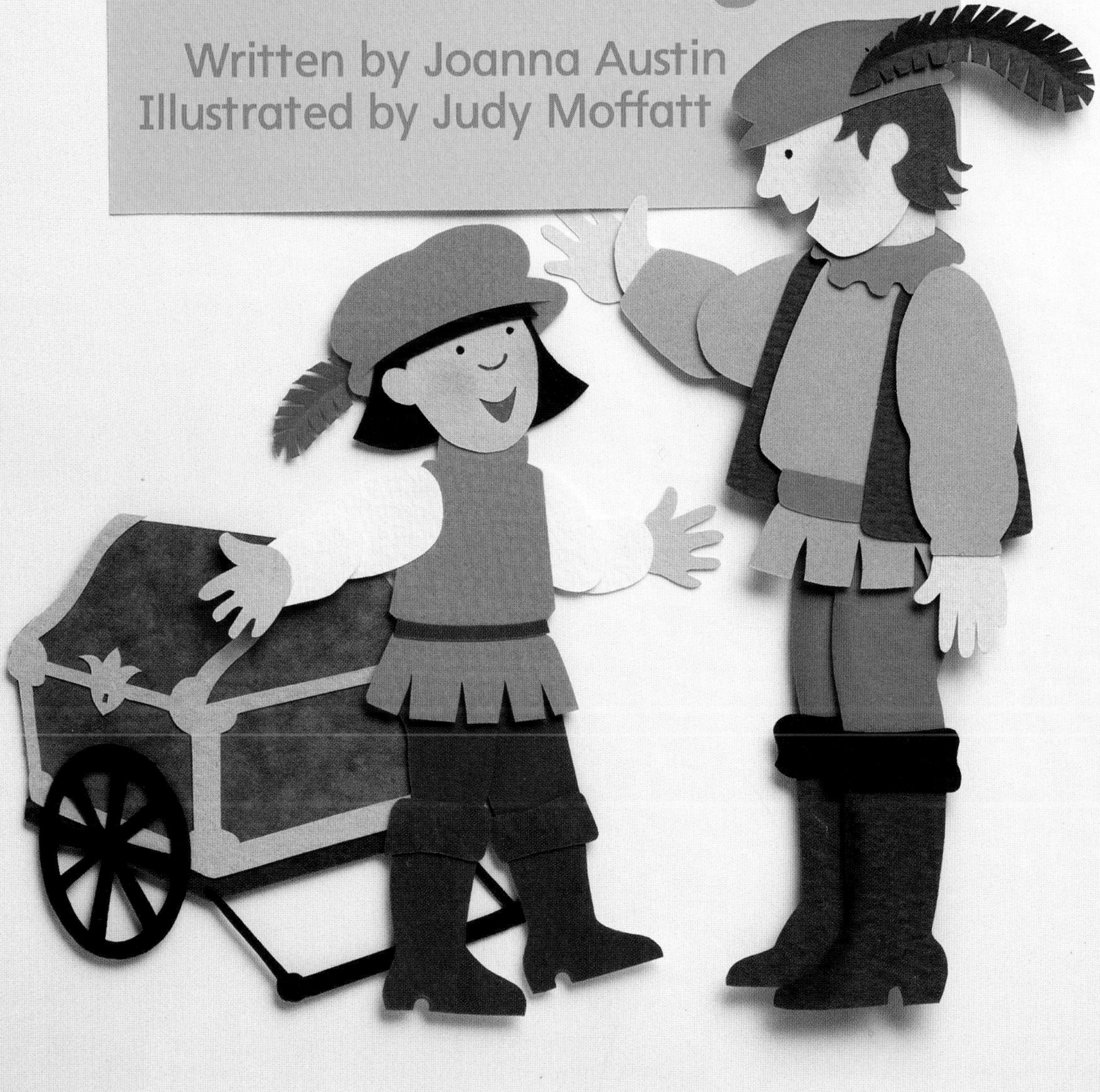

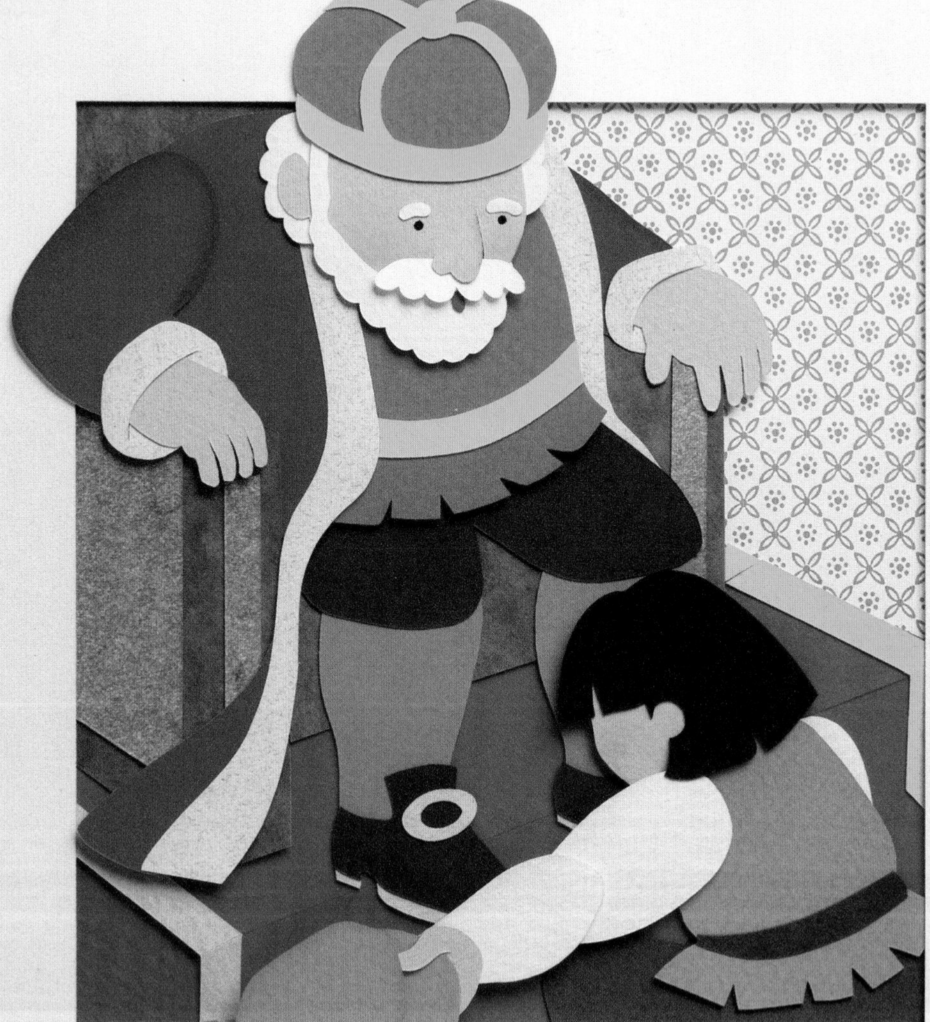

What did you bring?

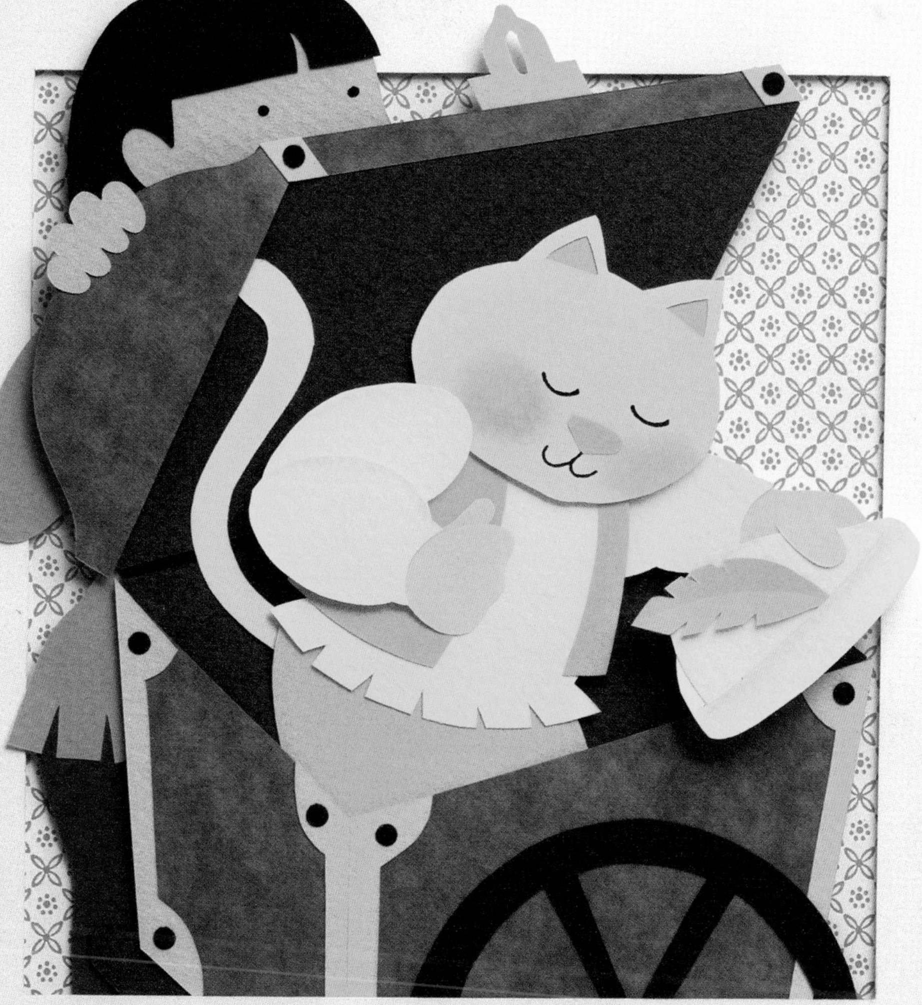

A yellow cat,

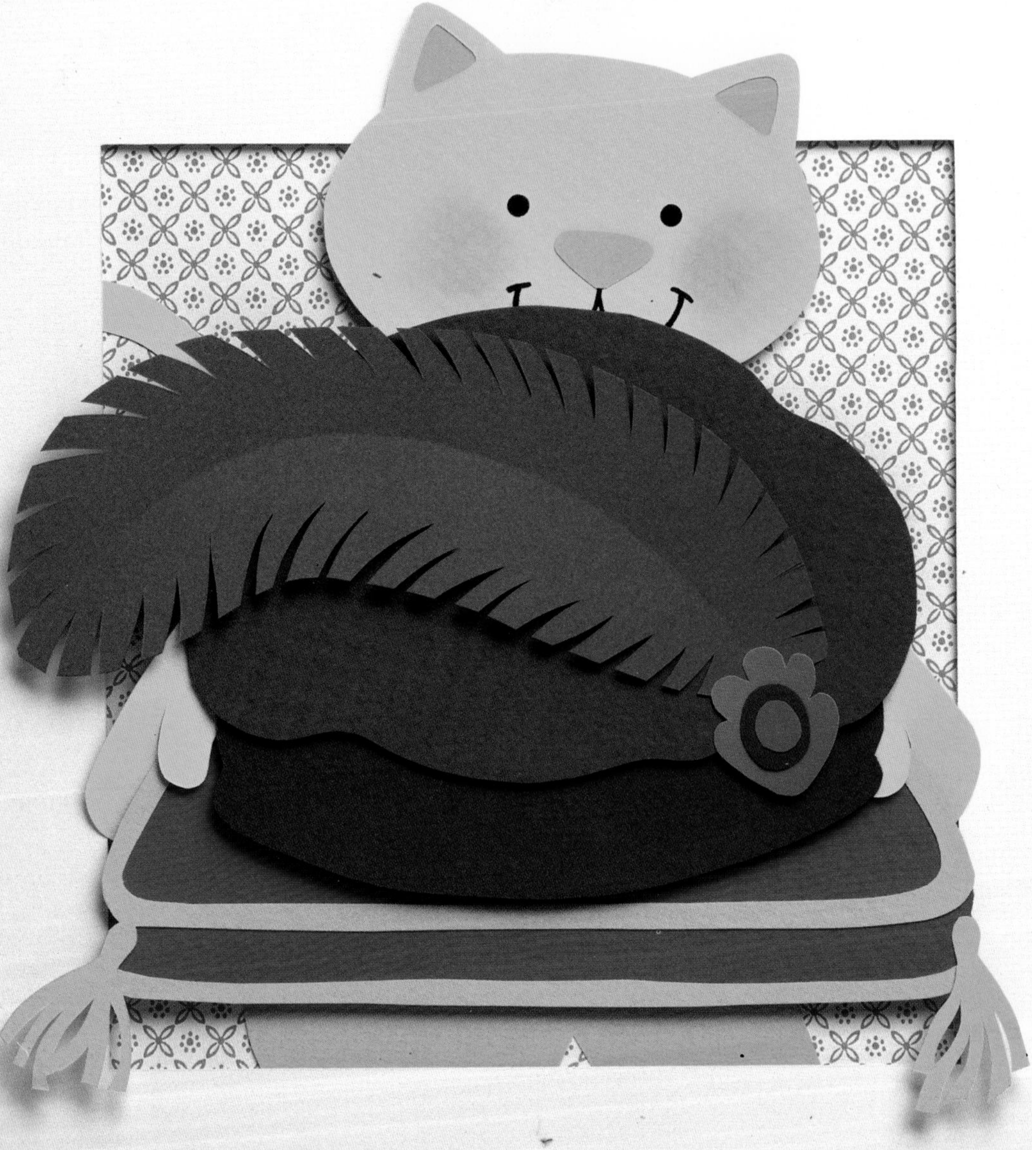

a blue hat,

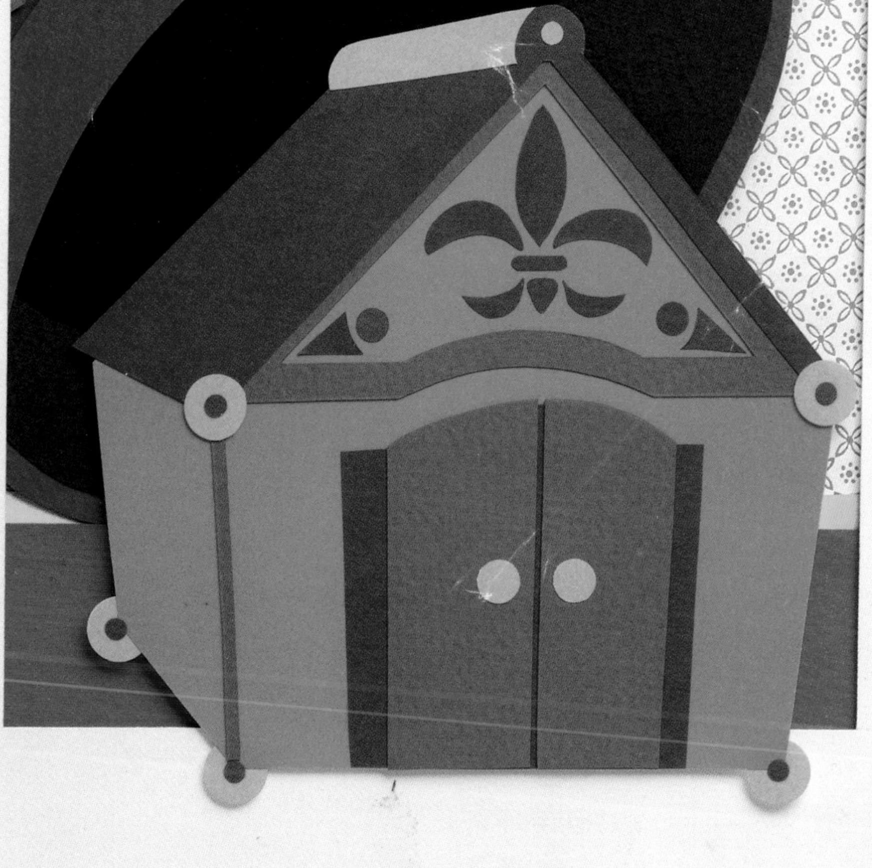

a green house,

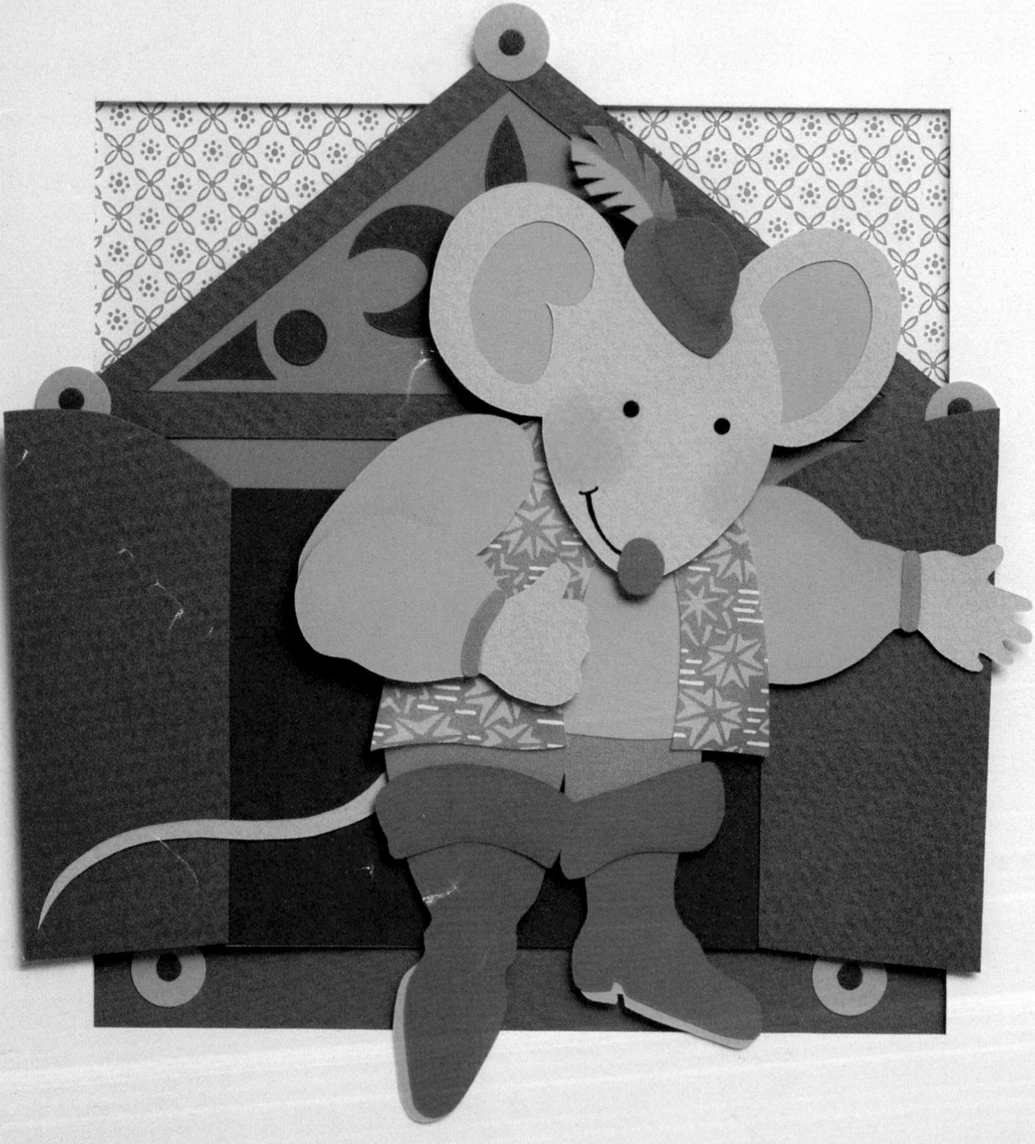

a pink mouse,

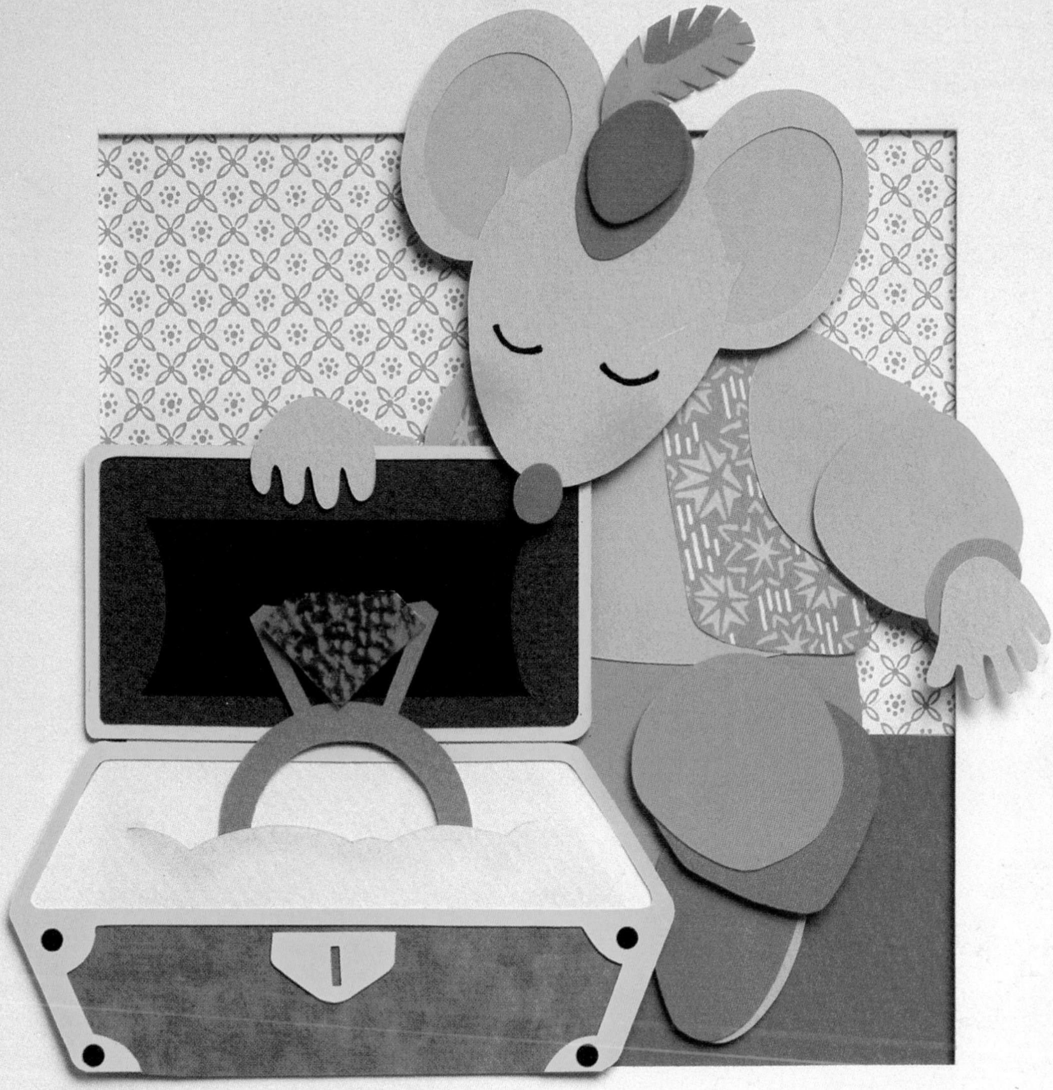

and a red ring . . .

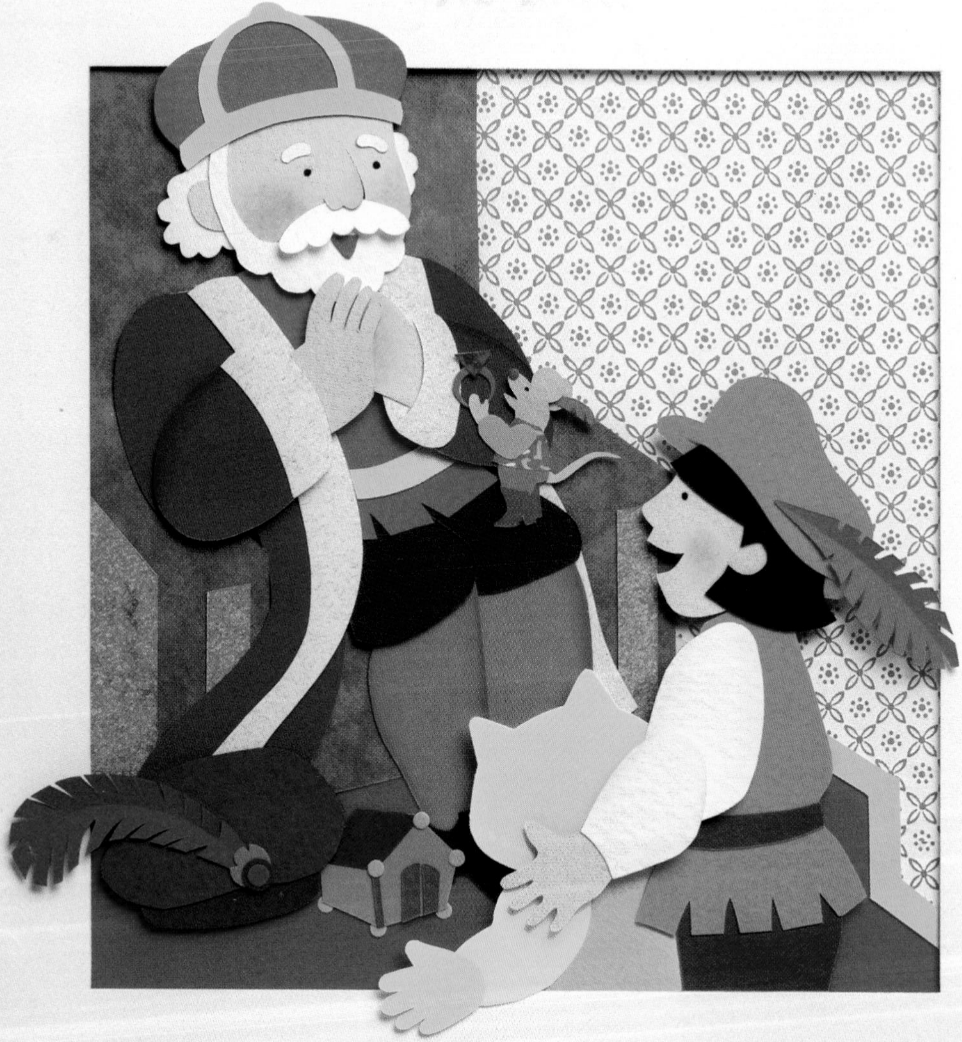

for the king!